Halloween Spooky Makes

By L.T. Marshall

Welcome to my Knitting Designs.

By L.T. Marshall

I have been creating knitting patterns for many years for my own benefit and finally decided to write them down for sale. I occasionally share free patterns on my website.
I would say they're suitable for someone with intermediate skill, although a beginner may be able to do just as well with a little more time and patience.
Have fun creating these collectible characters for your family and friends.
You can find my creations online under the name One Creative Family, although I am now an author by the name L.T.Marshall. I have a YouTube channel under my new brand - One Creative Family..

WWW.LTMarshall.Blog

ISBN - 9798648370364

Contents

By L.T. Marshall

Welcome to my Knitting Designs.

By L.T. Marshall

Safety guidelines

The items in these patterns are not suitable for babies and very young children.

Knitting yarns

Double knitting in various colours, as stated in the instructions.

Abbreviations

P - Purl. P1 - Purl one. Pwise - Purl Wise.

K - Knit. K1 - Knit one. Kwise - Knit Wise

Sts - stitches,

K2 tog - Knit 2 Together. P2 tog - Purl 2 Together.

Inc 1 - Increase 1 stitch by knitting in the front and back of stitch. Y.Fwd - Yarn forward around needle. St-st - Stocking Stitch. G-st - Garter stitch, Slp1 - slip one stitch to the other needle without working.

B+T tightly - Break off yarn leaving a long end and thread it through stitches left on knitting needle, pull together tightly then fasten off.

Additional instructions - for some of the detailing you will need to be able to make a chain stitch.

Needles (unless additional sizes stated)

UK sized 10 and 12 - USA sized 3.25mm and 2.5mm

Walter Werewolf

Knitted in DK Wool

For This Project - You need.

Knitting yarns.

Fawn, Black and white
Fur like wool in browns. We used scarf yarn

Additional materials.

Toy eyes or black felt ovals
Toy Stuffing – Small bag.
Pink Sharpie to blush cheeks

Tools.

No.10 needles. UK sized or 3.25mm
Wool needle. UK sized
Sewing needle.
Scissors.

Walter Werewolf

Legs (Make 2)

In fawn and size 10 needles
Cast on 10sts
Incl into every st (20sts)
Starting with a P row, Stst 6 rows
Join fur colour
(P1, P2tog) to last st, P1
K1 row
Stst 20 rows
Leave on a spare needle and make second leg the same way

Body

Put both legs on one needle, with work facing you.
In fawn, knit across both legs to join them
P 1 row
(K2, Incl) to end
Stst 9 rows
Join Fur
(K4, K2tog) to end
Stst 5 rows
(K1, K2tog) to end
P 1 row
Join Fawn (Main body colour)
(K1, Incl) to end (this is the start of the head)
P 1 row
K2, Incl) to end (40sts)
Stst 20 rows
(P2, P2tog) to end
(K1, K2tog) to end
(P2tog) to end
B+T

To make up

Starting at head, draw up tightly and over stitch seam right down center of doll at back, using colours left hanging.

Fasten off each colour securely.

Stop where legs meet and stuff.

Join legs at center of crotch area and sew down each leg, stuff from base of foot being sure to stuff extra at boot toes and sew underneath in a straight seam from toe to heel.

With matching wool, loosely in-out stitch around the neck and draw up to create a more sturdy neckline. The eyebrows are chain stitched over eyes using the fur wool.

If using Toy eyes, make sure you insert them before stuffing and closing the head.

Arms (Make 2)

In fawn, cast on 8sts
Incl into every st
Starting P, Stst 5 rows
Join fur
(K1, K2tog) to end
P 1 row
Join Fawn
Stst 12 rows
(P2tog) to last st, P1
B+T

To make up

Draw thread tightly and sew down to cast on edge, stuff well.
Join to body as pictured.

Muzzle

Cast on 20 Sts on No.10 needles in fawn
Stst 5 rows
(P2tog) to end
(K2tog) to end
B+T

To make up

Sew down from gathered end to Cast on edge, leaving base open. Stuff and
sew directly to toys face as pictured. The nose is a V shape in black wool and stitches make up his fangs in white wool. Blush cheeks.

Ears (make 2)

cast on 20sts in fawn
Stst 3 rows
(P1, P2tog) to end
K 1 row
(P1, P2tog) to end
K 1 row
(P2tog) to end
B+T

Sew from B+T down seam to cast on edge, move seam to middle back and flatten. Sew base shut. Pinch the ear in the center and sew to keep shape before applying to head as pictured.

Walter Werewolf

Side burns (make 2)

In fur, cast on 5 sts
K 1 row
Cast off

To make up

These are sewn directly under the ear and down side of face to mimic side burns for our hair werewolf.

Tail

Cast on 8sts in Lime green
Stst 4 rows
(K3, Incl) to end
Stst 3 rows
(K2, Incl) to end
Stst 3 rows
(K1, Incl) to end
Stst 3 rows
P 1 row
(K3, K2tog) to end
P 1 row
(K2, K2tog) to end
P 1 row
(K1, K2tog) to end
P 1 row
(K2tog) to end
(P2tog) to end
B+T

To make up

Sew from tip, up seam to cast on edge, joining sides. Stuff and sew to toys rump.

Raymond Rat

Knitted in DK Wool

For This Project - You need.

Knitting yarns.

DK wool in Fawn and dusky pink

Additional materials.
Toy eyes and a scrap of white wool. Pink sharpie marker for blushing cheeks.

Tools.

I use size 10 knitting needles and size 12 (UK sized)
Wool needle.
Sewing needle.
Scissors.

Raymond Rat

The body and head. (One piece)

Cast on 4sts fawn on No.10 needles
Incl KW into every st (8sts)
P 1row
Incl KW into every st (16sts)
P1 row
Incl KW into every st (32sts)
P 1 row
Stst 10 rows
(K2, K2tog) to end (24sts)
St st 15 rows
(K1, K2tog) to end
P 1 row
(K1, Incl) to end
St st 5 rows
(K2, Incl) to last st, K1
St st 3 rows
(K1, K2tog) to end
P 1 row
(K1, K2tog) to last 2 sts, K2
P 1 row
(K1, K2tog) to end
P 1 row
(K1, K2tog) to end (5sts)
P 1 row
K2tog, K1, K2tog
P3 tog
B+T

Ears (Make 2)

On No.12 needles
Cast on 10sts
Ststs 4 rows
(K2tog) to end
B+T

Raymond Rat

Front feet Make 2)

Cast on 8sts in fawn with no. 10 needles
Stst 4 rows
(K1, K2tog) to last
With Pink and using a no.12 needle
P 1 row
Now use both no. 12 needles
Stst 4 rows
(K2tog) to end
B+T

Back feet (make 2)

With no 12 needles and pink
Cast on 6sts
Stst 6 rows
(K2tog) to end
B+T

Tail

With Fawn and no 10 needles Cast on 4sts
Stst 2 rows
Switch to no.12 needles and join pink
Stst 35 rows
P2tog, twice
B+T

Raymond Rat

To make up

Body - Stitch from B+T end, stuffing as you go until you get to the base. Gather and sew closed. If you are using toy eyes, then add them in the face before stuffing.

Ears - Gather the B+T and sew to cast on edge. Move sew seam to back and flatten ear. Stitch base closed flat. Then stitch two bottom corners together to fold ear as pictured. Sew to head in desired position.

Legs- All legs are sewn from B+T end to cast on edge, only the fawn areas are stuffed. the pink are not. Gather open ends and sew to rat as pictured.

Tail - Sew the sail shut and only stuff where the fawn is used, sew to bum off rat as pictured.

Toes - For the little toes on each foot chain stitch 2 sts per toe, sewing in place as you go.

Face - To make the nose, mouth and teeth, I chain stitched the details of a V nose and upside down larger V with pink wool. To make the teeth I chain stitched 3 sts, folded in half and sewed in place.

Willow Witch

For This Project - You need.

Knitting yarns

Double knitting in -
Black, white (we used glitter wool)
Grey, Flesh, Green
Dk purple, Med purple and pink-purple
Orange
Brown and Fawn

Additional materials
Toy safety eyes in 4mm black
Stuffing – small amounts.

Tools

No.10 needles. UK sized
Wool needle.
Sewing needle.
Scissors.
Sharpie in pink for blushed cheeks

Willow Witch

Body and head (Made in one piece.)

With light grey and No.10 needles, cast on 10 Sts.
KW incl into each stitch (20 Sts).
P1 row.
(K1, Incl) to end (30 Sts).
St-St 6 rows. (start P) ~~K3 A~~
To shape top of fairys bottom.
Next row (P2 tog, 5 times) P10 (P2 tog, 5 times) ✓
K 1 row. ✗
Join on bodice colour (Black) work as follows.
P1 row ✗
K8, join on pink-purple and K4, Back to black K8 ✗
P8 black, Purple pink, P4, P8 black ✗
Repeat last 2 rows five times more ~~X3 P4 5~~
K 1 black row and continue in black only ✗
Next row - K3 (K2tog, 3 times) K2 (K2tog, 3 times) K3. ✗
St-st 2 rows ✗
Join on flesh
K1 row ✗
P1 row ✗

To shape head

Next row – (K1, Incl) to end ✗
St-st 14 rows ~~XXXXXXXXXXXX~~
(P2tog) to last st, P1
(K2tog) to last st, K1
B+T Tightly

To make up

Draw up thread tightly and sew down back seam until colour changes.
Stuff the head.. Sew up bodice and stuff, then sew up panties to cast on
stitches and stuff, making sure to fill out hips and bottom. Sew across cast
on stitches to close.
Thread a piece of wool through stitches around the neck line and draw up
firmly. Tie off and sew into back to hide threads to create neck.
Chain stitch black up each side of the pink purple Bodice panel to neaten
the edges. Then using Purple sew a criss cross pattern across the panel as
pictured.

13

Willow Witch

Right leg

Cast on 9 Sts in Dk Purple with No.10 needles.
P1 row.
Incl KW into each st (18 Sts).
St-st 3 rows.
Join on light grey and work as follows.
Stst 2 rows ✓
Join black
K2 (K2tog, 5 times) K6. ✓
P1 row ✗
Continue in 2 rows grey, 2 rows black for rest of leg.
K2 (K2tog, 3 times) K5. ✓
St-st 25 rows in stripes
P2tog to end
B+T

To make up

Sew across cast off edge and down seam stuffing as you go. Change colours to match knitted piece, sewing down to cast on edge. Stuff foot then sew along underneath to create shoe.

Left leg

Cast on 9 Sts in Dk Purple with No.10 needles.
P1 row.
Incl KW into each st (18 Sts).
St-st 3 rows. ✗
Join on light grey and work as follows.
Stst 2 rows ✗
Join black
K6 (K2tog, 5 times) K2. ✗
P1 row ✗
Continue in 2 rows grey, 2 rows black for rest of leg.
K5 (K2tog, 3 times) K2. ✗
St-st 25 rows in stripes
P2tog to end
B+T

14

To make up

Follow instructions for right leg, sew both legs side by side to the panties cast on edge.
To add the shoe details, chain stitch from center back of where purple shoe ends, come around front of foot and cross to other side of the shoe, fasten off and rejoin at opposite side of the shoe at the front, chain stitch across shoe creating a cross at front and around the back of foot to meet the starting point. Fasten off.

Arms (Make 2)

With Black cast on 4 Sts. (You will work 2 rows black, 2 rows grey until you change to flesh)
Incl KW into each st (8sts).
St-st 22 rows
Join flesh
Stst 6 rows
P2tog to last st, P1.
B+T tightly.

To make up

Pull thread tightly and sew down the seam, stuffing as you go to make it easier. Sew to cast on stitches then across these and gather to close.

15

Willow Witch

Leg Warmers (Make 2)

With orange cast on 15sts
St st 6 rows
Cast off

Sew warmer around Leg , just above the shoe, with seam at the back. For added detail i sewed 3 micro buttons on each warmer as pictured.

Sleeve (make 2)

Cast on 24sts in black
Stst 2 rows
K2tog to end
P 1 row
Incl into every st
StSt 3 rows
(P2tog) to end
(K2tog) to end
B+T

Cuff (make 2)

With white cast on 20sts
K1 row
(P2tog) to end
Cast off

To Make Up

The sleeve is gathered at the B+T and sewn down to the cast on edge.
Slide the sleeve over the end of the arm and secure at the top middle.
Then with an in out stitch around the indented part of the sleeve, gather around the arm and pull snugly. Sew in place.
The cuff is sewn around the wrist area on the grey stripe.
Then attach arm to side of the doll as pictured.

Willow Witch

Collar

With black cast on 20 sts
K 1 row ✓
K2tog, K8, K2tog, K7, K2tog
P 1 row
K2tog, K6, K2tog, K5, K2tog
Cast off PW

Top Skirt

With black cast on 30 Sts.
K1, Inc1 KW into each St ✗
P1 row. ✗
K1, Inc1, K to last 2 sts, Inc1, K1 ✗
Repeat the last two rows twice more ✗✗
P1 row ✗
K1, K2tog, K to last 3 sts, K2tog, K1 ✗
P1 row ✗
Repeat the last two rows until 39sts remain
(P2, P2tog) to last 3 sts, P3
K3, K2tog) to end
Cast off

To make up
This skirt is put on with seam to front, it stays wide open to reveal
underskirts and is sewn around the waist after the underskirts are sewn
on.

Second layer skirt

In white, cast on 60sts
Stst 2 rows
join orange
K1 row
White P 1 row
(P1, P2tog) to end, to create a border
P 1 white row (continue working stst for following rows)
Add Purple, K 1 row
White 2 rows
Green 1 row
White 1 row
White - (P1, P2tog) to end
(K3, K2tog) to end
Cast off

Underskirt

With purple-pink cast on 43 Sts.
K1, **Sl1, K4, turn
P4, turn
K5**
Repeat ** to ** along whole row to create scallop edge
Stst 16rows
(P1, P2tog) to end
Stst 7 rows
(P3, P2tog) to last st, P1
Cast off

To make up

Sew up skirts and put seams to the back. Slide the underskirt inside the second layer skirt and sew them together at the waist, position on doll and stitch around her waist before putting top layer skirt on.
If you have issue with the skirts curling up, then iron them before assembly or wash and pin flat to air dry.

Waist cord

Finger knit or chain stitch a cord 28cm long. fasten ends and tie around dolls waist as pictured.

Hat

Cast on 20sts in black
Stst 6 rows
K2tog, K to last 2 sts, K2tog
P1 row
Repeat last two rows until 2 sts remain
B+T

Hat Brim

Double up your wool for a stiff brim.
Cast on 25sts
K1 row
(K3, Incl) to last st, K1 ✓
K 1 row ✓
(K2, Incl) to last st, K1 ✓
K1 row ✓
(K1, Incl) to last st, K1
K 2 rows
Cast off

Hat Band

In orange cast on 25sts
Cast off

To Make up.

Sew hat seam up back to make a point. Stuff the base very lightly and sew to top of dolls head covering any hair strands you want to hide. Tuck them in. The brim is then laid around the hat and sewn in place, Stitch down at the back and around the rim a few places to anchor it down. The hat band sits around the hat on top of the brim as pictured.

Willow Witch

To make dolls hair

Cut Green wool into 30cm lengths.
Take 3 strands at a time and fold in half, sew the center fold to the dolls head along the center part from back of the head to the front, using chain stitch.
Pull the dolls hair to the sides of the face to make bunches and secure in place with stitching to the side of the head. Separate one bunch into two and twist to the end of the strands, Loosely pull behind the head to secure at back of the head and take the ends up on to the top of the head and sew down. These will be covered by the hat and hidden so do not need to be neat. Do the other side of the hair the same way. You will have what looks like a twist bun at the front which carries around behind the head and up inside the hat.

To finish the Doll

Blush the cheeks with pink sharpie marker and add eyes. If you use safety eyes they will need to have been inserted while assembling the head.

The broom

3 BBQ skewers cut to 19cm
With brown wool Cast on 40sts
K 4 rows
Cast off
Wrap this around the skewers lengthwise and sew shut around them to make the broom handle.

The bands

In dark brown
Cast on 12sts
Cast off

To add the brush.

Cut lengths of fawn wool, twice the length of how you want the broom to be.

20

Broom continued ....

Lay out flat and lay the broom handle in the center as pictured.

Gather with a length of wool and tie tight

Flip the wool down and tie another length of wool around the broom just near the fold, then another 1 cm below that. Sew the bands around the tied length.

For This Project - You need.

Knitting yarns.
Your chosen colour for the cat. We used black

Additional materials.
Scraps of felt in black and yellow for eyes
Grey wool or embroidery thread for details
Toy Stuffing – medium bag.
Ribbon to tie around his neck

Tools.

No.10 needles.
Wool needle.
Sewing needle.
Scissors.

Body & Head

Cast on 10 sts
- KW Inc1 into every stitch (20sts).
- PW Inc1 into every st (40sts).
- (K1, Inc1) to end (60sts).
- Starting with a P row St st 11 rows.
- (K4, K2tog) to end (50sts).
- P1 row.
- (K3, K2tog) to last st (40sts).
- P2 tog, P to last 2, P2tog (38sts).
- St st 4 rows.
- Next row -***K2tog, K to last 2 sts , K2tog (36sts).
- P1 row**.
- Repeat from *** to ** until 30 Sts remain, ending with a P row.
- Increase for the head as follows.
- K5, (Inc 1, K1) to last 5 Sts, K5 (40sts).
- P1 row (40 Sts).
- Repeat last 2 rows once more (55Sts).
- Next row - (K3, K2tog) to end (44sts).
- P1 row.
- Next row - (K2, K2tog) to end (33sts).
- P1 row.
- Next row - (K1, K2tog) to end (22sts).
- P2 tog to end (11sts).
- B+T tightly.

To make up

Sew from top of the head, down to where the neck is and stuff.
Draw a little wool through the increase for head row and pull tight for neck (using an in and out stitch around the neck and pulling a little tighter to draw in).Sew down body and stuff as you go until you close body completely.
Embroider the eyes on with black thread, stitching details in place.
The eyes are just a simple pointy ended oval with a stripe of black sewn on for the pupil.
Position as you prefer.

Front Legs (make 2)

Start at sole of foot - Cast on 8 Sts
- Inc K wise into every stitch (16sts).
- P1 row.
- (K1, inc1) to last 2 sts, K2 (23sts).
- P1 row.
- (K3, inc1) to last 3 sts, K3 (28sts).
- Start with K row, St st 4 rows.
- Next row - (K5, K2tog) to end (24sts)
- P1 row.
- Next row - (K4, K2tog) to end (20sts)
- P1 row.
- St st 11 rows.
- (P3, P2tog) to end
- Stst 9 rows
- (P2tog) to end.
- B+T tightly.

To make up

Sew from B+T down bottom of the leg , stuffing as you go. The foot base is gathered tight to close.
Wait until all 4 legs are made before sewing to the body so you can try positions to find the most desirable pose.

Back legs (make 2)

Start with the hand - Cast on 8 Sts
Inc K wise into every stitch (16sts).
P1 row.
(K1, incl) to last 2 sts, K2 (23sts).
P1 row.
(K3, incl) to last 3 sts, K3 (28sts).
P1 row.
Start with K row, St st 4 rows.
Next row - (K5, K2tog) to end (24sts).
P1 row.
Next row - (K4, K2tog) to end (20sts).
P1 row.
St st 8 rows.
(K3, K2tog) to end
St st 6 rows
(K2tog) to end.
B+T tightly.

To make up

Sew from B+T down bottom of the arm , stuffing as you go. The foot base
is gathered tight to close.

You can position and sew the arms and legs to the cats body in any
position you prefer, either sitting or standing.

Muzzle

Cast on 30 sts
- St st 4 rows.
- (K2, K2tog) to last 3 sts, K3 (27sts).
- P1 row.
- (K1, K2 tog) to lend (18sts).
- P1 row.
- (K2tog) to end (9 sts).
- B+T tightly

To make up

Sew from B+T end to cast on edge to make a domed muzzle. Turn right side out. Stuff and attach to face. Using grey yarn/thread embroider a nose and mouth.

Ears (make 2)

Cast on 20 sts (using colour A)
- St st 4 rows
- (K3, K2tog) to end
- P 1 row
- (K2, K2tog) to end
- P 1 row
- (K1, K2tog) to end
- P 1 row
- (K2tog) to end
- P 1 row
- B&T

To make up.

Sew from B&T joining side seams until you get to the cast on base. Move the seam to centre back and sew seam shut flat. This makes your pointy ear.
Pinch in the centre when sewing to head to help shape it and apply in desired position.

Tail.

Cast on 15 sts
Stst 40 rows
(K3tog) to end
B&T

To make up.
The tail is rolled into itself length ways rather than stuffing. Rolling it from the tip until you create a long sausage and secure the seam with stitches before sewing to cats rump.

I hope you enjoyed making our Halloween cat x

Puff the Dragon

Knitted in DK Wool

For This Project - You need.

Knitting yarns.

Main lime green
Dark green, medium green, light green (can be same as main body)
Red

Additional materials.

Embroidery thread in Black or toy eyes
Toy Stuffing – Small bag.
Pink Sharpie to blush cheeks

Tools.

No.10 needles. UK sized
Wool needle. UK sized
Sewing needle.
Scissors.

28

Puff the Dragon

Legs (Make 2)

In lime and size 10 needles
Cast on 10sts
Inc1 into every st (20sts)
Starting with a P row, Stst 6 rows
(P1, P2tog) to last st, P1
Stst 20 rows
Leave on a spare needle and make second leg the same way

Body ~~X23~~

Put both legs on one needle, with work facing you.
In dark green knit across both legs to join them
P 1 row
(K2, Inc1) to end
P 1 row dark green ✓
join Medium green and K 1 row ✓
Stst 3 rows ✓
Join light green
Stst 4 rows ✓
Join Dark green
(K4, K2tog) to end ✓
Stst 3 rows ✓
Join med green
Stst 2 rows ✓
(K1, K2tog) to end ✓
P 1 row ✓
Join Light green (Main body colour)
(K1, Inc1) to end (this is the start of the head) ✓
P 1 row ✓

Puff the Dragon

(K2, Incl) to end (40sts) ✓
Stst 20 rows
(P2, P2tog) to end ✓ 1 2 3 4 5 6 7 8 9 10 11 12 13 14 15 16 17 18 19 20
(K1, K2tog) to end
(P2tog) to end
B+T

To make up

Starting at head, draw up tightly and over stitch seam right down center of
doll at back, using colours left hanging.
Fasten off each colour securely.
Stop where legs meet and stuff.
Join legs at center of crotch area and sew down each leg, stuff from base of
foot being sure to stuff extra at boot toes and sew underneath in a straight
seam from toe to heel to create boot.
With medium green wool, loosely in-out stitch around the neck and draw
up to create a more sturdy neckline.
Fasten off.
If using Toy eyes , make sure you insert them before stuffing and closing
the head.

30

Puff the Dragon

Arms (Make 2)

In lime green, cast on 8sts
Incl into every st
Starting P, Stst 5 rows
(K1, K2tog) to end
Stst 10 rows
(P2tog) to last st, P1
B+T

To make up

Draw thread tightly and sew down to cast on edge, stuff well.
Join to body as pictured.

31

Puff the Dragon

Muzzle

Cast on 20 Sts on No.10 needles in lime green
Stst 5 rows
(P2tog) to end
(K2tog) to end
B+T

To make up

Sew down from gathered end to Cast on edge, leaving base open.Stuff and sew directly to Puffs face as pictured. If using toy eyes for nostrils apply them before sewing to face.

Horns (Make 2)

Cast on 6sts in dark green
K 1 row
(P1, P2tog) to end
K 1 row
(P2tog) to last st, P1
B+T

To Make Up

Sew down from gathered end to cast on edge, stuff very lightly and sew to head as pictured

Ears (make 2)

cast on 5sts in Lime green
Incl into every st - 10sts
Starting P, Stst 3 rows
K1, (Yfwd, K2tog) to last st, K1
Stst 3 rows
(K2tog) to end
Cast off

Fold the ear in half length ways so you create a picot edge, sew all seams closed and attach to dragons head as pictured.

Spikes

In red, cast on 50sts
P 1 row
K2, (yfwd, K2tog) to last 2 sts, K2
P 1 row
Cast off

To make up

Fold the ridge in half length ways to create a long picot edge. This is sewn from tail tip , up along the back and over the head to end between the eyes.

Tail

Cast on 15sts in Lime green
Stst 4 rows
(K3, K2tog) to end
Stst 3 rows
(K2, K2tog) to end
Stst 3 rows
(K1, K2tog) to end
Stst 3 rows
(K2tog) to end
P 1 row
B+T

To make up

Sew from tip, up seam to cast on edge, joining sides. Stiff and sew to dragons rump.

Puff the Dragon

Wings (Make 2)

In Dark green cast on 10sts
K 1 row ✓
K8, Inc1, K1 ✗
K 1 row ↓
K9, Inc1, K1 ✗
K 1 row ↓
K10, Inc 1 , K1 ✗
K 2 rows ↓
Cast off 5sts, K to end ✗
K 5 rows ✓
Cast off 5 sts, K to end
K 5 rows
Cast off

To Make up

The wing is detail with chain stitch in red as pictured, to give definition.
Once you chain stitch, turn the piece over and stitch in a zig zag through
the visible red stitches to join them and neaten the reverse. The wings are
made to look symmetrical so be aware of which side to sew when making
the pair and sew to the body as pictured. I sewed only half the wing height
to the body so the lower half looks like part of the wing shape.

Blush cheeks with Pink sharpie marker and use red wool to stitch details of
claws on hands and feet.

34

Pumpkins

Knitted in DK Wool

For This Project - You need.

Knitting yarns.

orange or cream
Brown
Green

Additional materials.

Toy Stuffing – Small bag.

Tools.

No.10 and 12 needles. UK sized
Wool needle.
Sewing needle.
Scissors.

Pumpkins

Small Pumpkin

In burnt orange and size 10 needles
Cast on 10sts
Inc1 into every st (20sts)
P 1 row
(Inc1, K1 , Inc1, P1) to end
P 1 row
(Inc1, K3, Inc1, P1) to end
P 1 row
(Inc1, K5 , Inc1, P1) to end
P 1 row
(Inc1, K7 , Inc1, P1) to end
P 1 row
(Inc1, K9 , Inc1, P1) to end
P 1 row
(K13, P1) to end
P 1 row
(K13, P1) to end
P 1 row
(K2tog, K9 , K2tog, P1) to end
P 1 row
K2tog, K7 , K2tog, P1) to end
P 1 row
K2tog, K5 , K2tog, P1) to end
P 1 row
K2tog, K3, K2tog, P1) to end
P 1 row
K2tog, K1 , K2tog, P1) to end
P 1 row
(K2tog) to end
(P2tog) to end
B+T

Pumpkins

Large Pumpkin

In Cream and size 10 needles

Cast on 10sts
Incl into every st (20sts)
P 1 row
Incl into every st - 40sts
P 1 row
(Incl, K5 , Incl, P1) to end
P 1 row
(Incl, K7, Incl, P1) to end
P 1 row
(Incl, K9, Incl, P1) to end
P 1 row
(Incl, K11 , Incl, P1) to end
P 1 row
(Incl, K13, Incl, P1) to end
P 1 row
(Incl, K15, Incl, P1) to end
P 1 row
(**(K19, P1) to end
P 1 row***
Repeat from ** to *** three more times
(K2tog, K15 , K2tog, P1) to end
P 1 row
K2tog, K13 , K2tog, P1) to end
P 1 row
K2tog, K11 , K2tog, P1) to end
P 1 row
K2tog, K9, K2tog, P1) to end
P 1 row
K2tog, K7 , K2tog, P1) to end
P 1 row
K2tog, K5 , K2tog, P1) to end

Pumpkins

P 1 row
K2tog, K3 , K2tog, P1) to end
P 1 row
K2tog, K1 , K2tog, P1) to end
P 1 row
(K2tog) to end
(P2tog) to end
B+T

To make up

Starting at B+T end and sew down , joining side seams until you get two thirds of the way down to leave yourself a hole to stuff. Stuff well and close to the base, gather stitches of cast on edge and close tightly.
You will have a round flattish shape. Push a needle from center middle bottom, up to center middle of the top - drawing wool through, and then sew back down to bottom. Pull tight and tie. This will indent the base and top as pictured.
Next you will use the lines created by your P sts to sew in and out, from base to top and draw slightly tight to pull in the separation lines. This will create the pumpkin shape.

38

Pumpkins

Stems

Small

In Brown and no . 10 needles
Cast on 8sts
Stst 5 rows
(K2tog) to end
B+T

Large

In brown and no. 10 needles
Cast on 10sts
Stst 8 rows
(K2tog) to end
B+T

To make up

Gather from B+T end and sew to cast on base. Only stuff the larger stems before sewing in place on the center top of the pumpkin as pictured.

Pumpkins

Leaves

Small

In green and no.10 needles
Cast on 5sts
Incl into every st - 10sts
Stst 3 rows
K2tog, K6, K2tog
P 1 row
K2tog, K4, K2tog
P 1 row
(K2tog) to end
(K3tog) to end
B+T

Large

Cast on 10sts
Incl into every st - 20sts
Stst 7 rows
(K2tog, K16, K2tog)
P 1 row
K2tog, K14, K2tog)
P 1 row
K2tog, K12, K2tog)
P 1 row
(K2tog) to end
(P2tog) to end
(K2tog)
B+T

To Make Up

Sew from gathered B+T end to cast on edge, joining seams, Move seam to middle back of leaf and flatten, Sew base closed. Gather base and sew in place as pictured.

Pumpkins

Vines

Small

In green and with no.12 needles
Cast on 20sts
Cast off

Large

In green and no. 10 needles
Cast on 30sts
Cast off

To make up

The piece will curl by itself but you can shape it accordingly. Sew one end to the pumpkin top center as pictured and leave laying over the edge of the pumpkin as a vine.

Batty Bat

Knitted in DK Wool

For This Project - You need.

Knitting yarns.

Black
Grey
Another shade of grey or fur wool for the belly.
We used glitter grey.

Additional materials.

Toy eyes
Toy Stuffing – Small bag.
Pink Sharpie to blush cheeks

Tools.

No.10 needles. UK sized
Wool needle. UK sized
Sewing needle.
Scissors.

Legs (Make 2)

In Normal Grey
Cast on 7 sts
Incl into every st - 14sts
Stst 10 rows

Leave on a spare needle and make second leg the same way

Body

Put both legs on one needle, with wrong side facing you.
In Glitter Grey, P across both legs to join them - 28sts
Stst 12 rows
(K3, K2tog) to end
Stst 4 rows
(P2, P2tog) to end
Stst 4 rows
Join Normal Grey
Incl into every st
Stst 19 rows
(K2tog) to end
(P2tog) to end
B+T

Batty Bat

(**To make up**

Starting at head, draw up tightly and over stitch seam right down center of doll at back, using colours left hanging.
Fasten off each colour securely.
Stop where legs meet and stuff.
Join legs at center of crotch area and sew down each leg, stuff from base of foot being sure to stuff extra at boot toes and sew underneath in a straight seam from toe to heel.
With matching wool, loosely in-out stitch around the neck and draw up to create a more sturdy neckline. The eyebrows are chain stitched over eyes using the fur wool.
If using Toy eyes, make sure you insert them before stuffing and closing the head.

Muzzle

In normal Grey
Cast on 15sts
Stst 5 rows
(P3tog) to end
B+T

To make up

From B+T end pull tight and sew down to cast on edge. Stuff and sew to bat's face in the front center as pictured.

44

Arms (Make 2)

In Normal Grey
Cast on 10sts
STst 5 rows
P2tog, P6, P2tog
Stst 5 rows
P2tog, P4, P2tog
Stst 5 rows
P2tog, P2, P2tog
Stst 5 rows
P2tog, twice
B+T

To make up

Draw thread tightly and sew down to cast on edge, stuff only the very end lightly to retain shape. Flatten the end and sew seam shut.
Join to body as pictured after wings are sewn on.

Ears (Make 2)

In Normal Grey
Cast on 4sts
Incl into every st - 8sts
Stst 3 rows
(K1, K2tog) to end
P 1 row
(K2tog) to end
B+T

To make up

Gather tightly and sew down joining seams, move the seam to middle back and flatten the ear. Sew in place to the bats head as pictured.

Muzzle

Cast on 20 Sts on No.10 needles in fawn
Stst 5 rows
(P2tog) to end
(K2tog) to end
B+T

To make up

Sew down from gathered end to Cast on edge, leaving base open. Stuff and sew directly to toys face as pictured. The nose is a V shape in black wool and stitches make up his fangs in white wool. Blush cheeks.

Wings (Make 2

In Black
Cast on 30sts
K 1 row
K28, Inc1, K1
K 1 row
K29, Inc1, K1
K 1 row
K30, Inc1, K1
K 1 row
K31, Inc1 , K1
K 1 row
K32, Inc1, K1
**Cast off 5sts, K to end
Stst 5 rows***
Repeat from ** to *** until you have only 5sts left, work the 5 stst rows and cast off those last 5.

To Make up

The wing is sewn to the side of the bat, in the center of the side from neck to base of foot as pictured. Once sewn in place the arm is sewn in front of the top of the wing. Sewn along the top of the wing to join and the remaining wing is chain stitched to add detail.
Sew the bottom of the arm to the wing also, with it flattened as picture so it gives the wing stability. Finish the wing by chain stitching as pictured to create a bat win.
On the reverse sew in and out through the visible stitched in a zig zag motion to connect them and neaten.

Blush the bats cheeks with sharpie. I used toy eyes for the eyes and the nostrils, but you can use sewing thread or wool.

Twooty the owl

Knitted in DK Wool

For This Project - You need.

Knitting yarns.

Lemon, Pink
Purple
Turquoise and light turquoise
Burnt ornage

Additional materials.

Embroidery thread in Black or toy eyes
Toy Stuffing – Small bag.

Tools.

No.10 needles. UK sized
Wool needle. UK sized
Sewing needle.
Scissors.

Twooty the owl

Starting in Lemon, cast on 9sts
P 1 row
Incl into every st (18sts)
P 1 row
Incl into every st
Join pink
P 1 row
(K2, Incl) to end
Stst 2 rows
Join Lemon
Stst 4 rows
Join Pink
Stst 4 rows
Join Lemon
Stst 3 rows
(K4, K2tog) to end
Join Pink
Stst 2 rows
Join Purple
Stst 7 rows
(K1, K2tog) to end
P 1 row
Slp1, K9, turn
Slp1, P8, turn
K15,Slp1, K8, Slp1, turn
K12
Cast off

53

To make up

The ears are made by joining the side simes at the top, then move the join to centre back and flatten piece. Sew along top line of piece joining back and front.
The sew down the seam at the back , joining the sides together and stuff as you go. Gather bottom and close.

Twooty the owl

In Orange
Cast on 4 sts
K1, (Incl) to end
Stst 3 rows
K2, (Yfwd, K2tog) to last st, K1
Stst 3 rows
(K2tog) to end
Cast off

To make up

Fold in half along pattern line which creates a picot edge. Sew all seams together then sew to base of body as pictured.

Beak

Cast on 10sts in orange
(K3, K2tog) to end
(P2, P2tog) to end
(K1, K2tog) to end
(P2tog) to end
B&T

To make up

Sew from gathered end to cast on edge, Move seam to center back and flatten beak. Sew the opening shut and sew to owls face.

Eyes

Cast on 15 Sts on No.10 needles in Turquoise
Join light turquoise
P 1 row
(K2tog) to end
B+T

To make up

Pull the B+T tight to pull work into a circle. Sew edge seams together and sew to owls face as pictured.

Wings (make 2)

Cast on 6sts in cream
K 1 row
Incl into every st
P 1 row
K 1 row
P1, P2tog to last 3 sts, P2tog, P1
Repeat these last 2 rows until 3 sts remain
K1 row
B+T

To Make Up

Flatten out and sew ends in. Place on side of owl and sew in place as pictured

Twooty the owl

Cats on 10 sts
Incl into every st
Stst 3 rows
K2 (yfwd, K2tog) to end
Stst 3 rows
(K2tog) to end
Cast off.

To make up

Fold in half along pattern line and sew all seams together. Sew to owls behind as pictured

57

Autumn, Dinky Doll

Knitted in DK Wool

For This Project - You need.

Knitting yarns.

Flesh
Mustard, Pumpkin orange, Tan, Burnt orange, Medium red, Burgundy,
Milk chocolate brown
Dark brown for hair and boots

Additional materials.

Embroidery thread in Black or toy eyes
Toy Stuffing – Small bag.
Pink Sharpie to blush cheeks

Tools.

No.11 needles. UK sized
Wool needle. UK sized
Sewing needle.
Scissors.

Autumn, Dinky Doll

Legs (Make 2)

In darkest brown and no. 11 needles
Cast on 5sts
Incl into every st - 10sts
Stst 4 rows, starting P
K 1 row
Join mustard colour
K 1 row
Stst 9 rows
Leave on a spare needle and make an identical second leg

Body

Put both legs onto one needle with wrong side of work facing you
Using pumpkin orange
P across both legs to join
Stst 2 rows
Join tan
Stst 3 rows
Join Burnt orange
Stst 2 rows
(P3, P2tog) to end
Join Red
Stst 3 rows
Join Burgundy
(P2, P2tog) to end
Stst 2 rows
Join Choc brown
Stst 2 rows
(K1, K2tog) to end
Join Flesh
P 1 row
Incl in every st
P 1 row
(K1, Incl) to end
Stst 5 rows
Join mustard
Stst 4 rows
(K2tog to end
P2tog to end
B+T

59

To make up

Starting at head, draw up tightly and over stitch seam right down center of doll at back, using colours left hanging.

Fasten off each colour securely.

Stop where legs meet and stuff.

Join legs at center of crotch area and sew down each leg, stuff from base of foot being sure to stuff extra at boot toes and sew underneath in a straight seam from toe to heel to create boot.

With medium green wool, loosely in-out stitch around the neck and draw up to create a more sturdy neckline.

Fasten off.

If using Toy eyes , make sure you insert them before stuffing and closing the head.

Autumn, Dinky Doll

Jumper Hem

In Pumpkin orange
Cast on 24sts
Cast off

To make up

This is laid around the legs to hide where they join to the doll. Leave some of the Pumpkin showing on the doll body and sew the top edge to the doll only, to turn the outfit into a jumper dress as pictured.

Roll neck

Cast on 15sts in Chocolate brown
Cast off.

To make up

This is wrapped around the neck to create a turtle neck, Sewn together at back and lightly stitched in place around the center.

Hat Brim

Cast on 30sts in Mustard
Cast off

To Make Up

The hair needs to be applied before the hat brim. Attach wool along the line where the flesh and mustard meet. Stitching on as neatly as you can around two thirds of the head, leaving the front clear for the face.
Sew hat brim over the top of the hair, joining the mustard of the hat by stitching the top edge in place.

Autumn, Dinky Doll

Arms

In Flesh
Cast on 4sts
Incl into every st - 8 sts
Stst 3 rows
Join Burgundy
Starting K, Stst 10 rows
(K2tog) to end
B+T

To make up

Sew from gathered end to cast on edge. Stuff very lightly as you go and sew to side of body in desired position.

Cuffs

Cast on 12 Sts in Burgundy
Cast off

To Make up

These sit around the wrists covering some of the flesh to make a delicate small hand, Secure at back and stitch in place.

Pom pom on hat

Chain stitch a Mustard length of 15 sts.
I looped mine into 3 even loops and joined them at the base with a couple of sts. I sewed to middle top of hat for a cute pom pom.

Printed in Great Britain
by Amazon